You Don't Need Words!

A book about ways people talk without words

by Ruth Belov Gross · *illustrated by* Susannah Ryan

Scholastic Inc.
New York Toronto London Auckland Sydney

This book was written in the Frederick Lewis Allen Room
of the New York Public Library. The author is grateful
to the Library for this privilege.

ISBN 0-590-43898-0

12 11 10 9 8 7 6 5 4 3 2 1 2 5 6 7 8 9/9 0/0

Printed in the U.S.A. 14

Design by Claire B. Counihan

The illustrations in this book
were done in sepia ink
and watercolor.

For WILLY,
with more and more love,
and for WRAGGLES
R.B.G.

For MICHAEL
S.R.

What would you do
if you wanted to say something
but you couldn't talk
and did not know how to write?

What would you do
if you went to a country
where nobody knew English?

What would you do
if you wanted to leave a message
for somebody who couldn't read?

You will find out some of the things
you could do when you read this book.
This book tells how people can say things
to each other and understand each other
without using words.

Sign language is a good way to talk to people when you don't know their language. When Christopher Columbus landed in America, he used sign language to talk to the Indians he met.

Columbus and the Indians probably pointed a lot and did other things that were easy to understand. They probably made up their own sign language as they went along.

These people are saying some things in sign language. Can you guess what they are saying?

Baby

Cold

Sleepy

Pretending to do something is the easiest kind of sign language to use. It is called *pantomime.*

Most kinds of sign language
are like regular languages.
You have to learn them.
But if you know one kind of sign language,
it is easier to understand another.

About a hundred years ago, some American Indians
visited a college for deaf people.
The deaf people had their own sign language,
and the Indians had theirs.

The Indians and the deaf people
were able to understand each other anyway.
They spent the day together and had a good time.

Here are some signs that deaf people
in America use. Each sign stands for
a whole word or for a thought.
In other countries, deaf people use
different signs for these words.
You will find more sign language on page 40.

Father
Tap your thumb
on the side of
your forehead.

Mother
Tap your thumb
on the side of
your chin.

I love you.
Point to yourself.
Cross your arms on your chest.
Then point to the person you love.

Deaf people also learn to make the letters of the alphabet with their fingers. That way, they can spell out hard words and names. Spelling with your fingers is called *finger-spelling.* When you finger-spell, though, you are really using words.

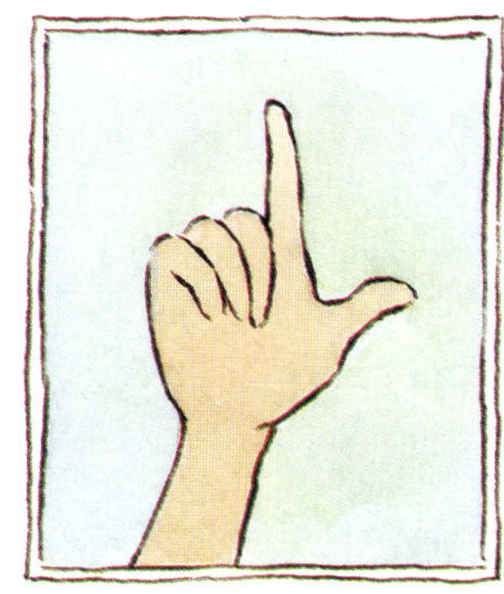
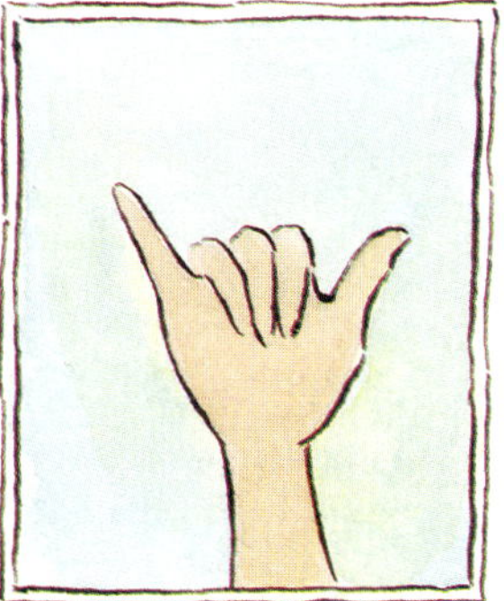

This is the way to make the letters I, L, and Y.

A quick way to say "I love you" is to make all three letters together.

When people talk about Indian sign language, they are really talking about the sign language of the Plains Indians. The Plains Indians used sign language more than any other Indians in America.

The Plains Indians lived on the grassy prairie lands called the Great Plains. They lived in tepees, hunted buffalo, rode fast horses, fought fierce battles, and didn't stay in one place very long.

There were once 25 or 30 tribes of Plains Indians — and they spoke more than 20 different languages. So very often, when two tribes got together, they couldn't understand each other. They had to use sign language instead.

Plains Indians also used sign language with members of their own tribe. They used it when they couldn't make any noise — when they were out hunting or on the warpath. Sometimes they used it just because they wanted to.

Nobody knows exactly why the Plains Indians started using sign language in the first place. Was it because they needed a way to talk to other tribes? Or was it because they had to keep quiet when they were hunting or fighting?

People who study sign language are still trying to decide which came first.

Some Indian signs are the same as the signs that deaf people use. Here are a few of them.

Love

Heavy

There is more Indian sign language on page 41.

Even if you do not know a special kind of sign language, you can use your hands and arms and the rest of your body to say things.

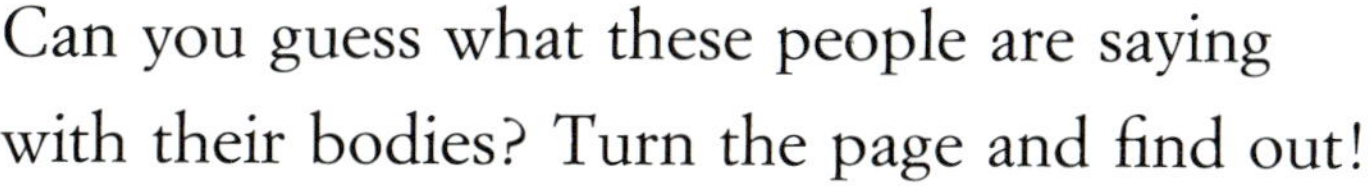

Can you guess what these people are saying with their bodies? Turn the page and find out!

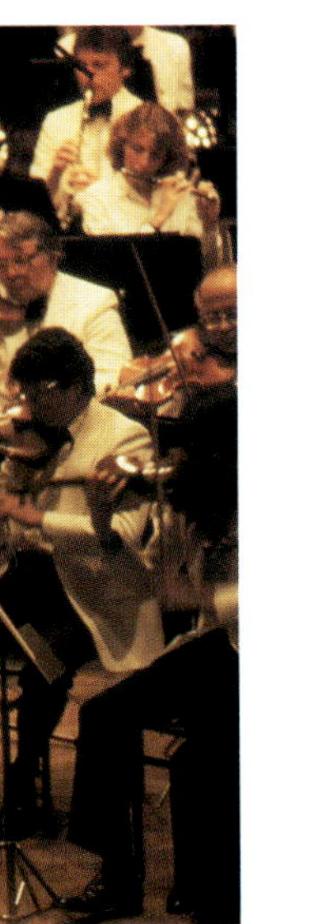

Bartholomew/Gamma-Liaison

Joan Farber

Leo Dewys/Everett C. Johnson

All of us talk with our bodies every day.
When you shake your head,
everyone knows you mean "no."
When you nod your head,
everyone knows you mean "yes."
Shaking your head and nodding your head
are both *gestures.*
Here are some gestures you probably know.
Turn the page for some more.

I'm strong.

What?

Blech! P.U. Fooey!

Some of these gestures are not very polite. People have used them for hundreds of years just the same.

People learn to use gestures
from the people around them.
So if you traveled around the world,
you would find that some gestures
were different from yours.

This is our gesture
for "please sit down."

And this is the gesture in Swaziland,
a country in Africa.

A mistake in sitting down
wouldn't be bad.
But you could get in trouble
if you pretended to cut your throat.
In Swaziland that means "I love you."

In most parts of the world, this is the way to say "please be quiet."

But in Ethiopia it is not polite to use this gesture — unless you are talking to children. For adults, you must put *four* fingers to your lips.

In some countries if you waved good-bye, people might think you were calling them over . . .

This is the gesture in Italy for "come here."

. . . and if you tried to call them over, they might think you were saying good-bye.

This is how people in Italy wave good-bye.

Have you ever looked at your mother's face when she was feeling very happy?
She did not have to tell you how she felt.
You just knew.
People do not have to say anything when they have strong feelings.
Their bodies and their faces tell you what they are feeling.

Even little babies show what they are feeling.
A team of scientists studied the faces
of angry babies, happy babies, sad babies,
and babies with other kinds of feelings.
They found out that for each kind of feeling
there is a special look on a baby's face.

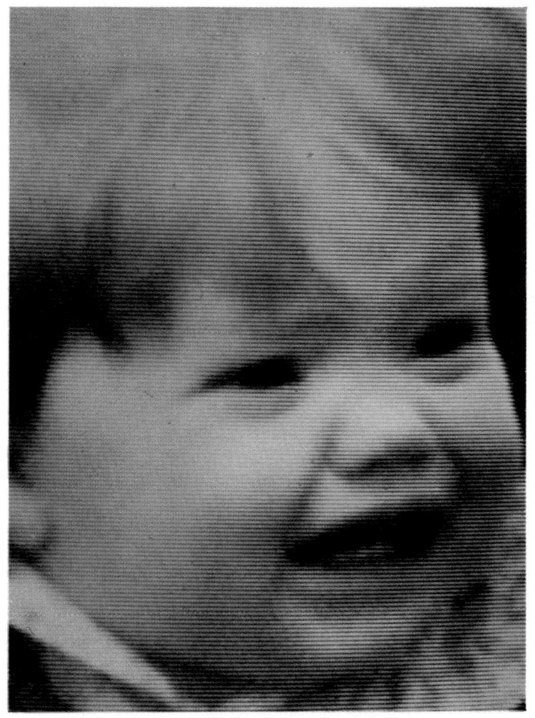

This baby is angry.

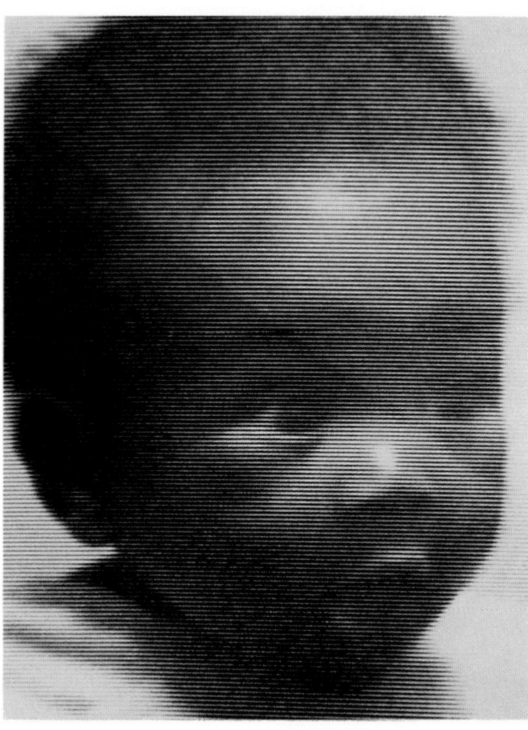

This baby has just had a surprise.

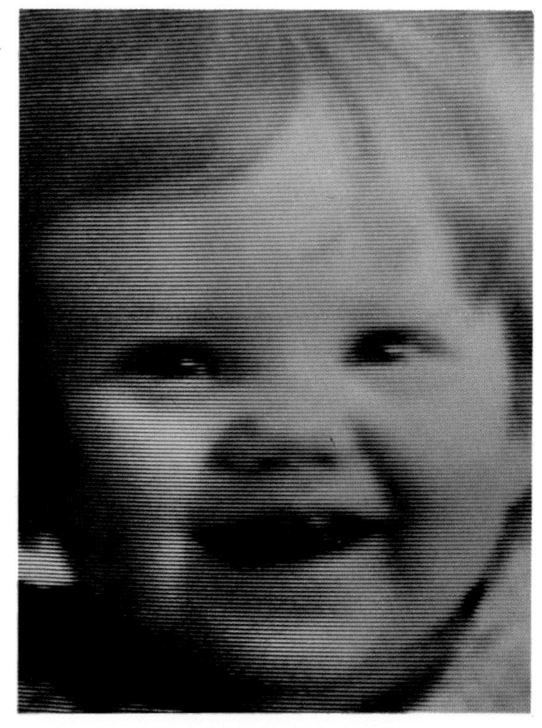

This baby is happy.

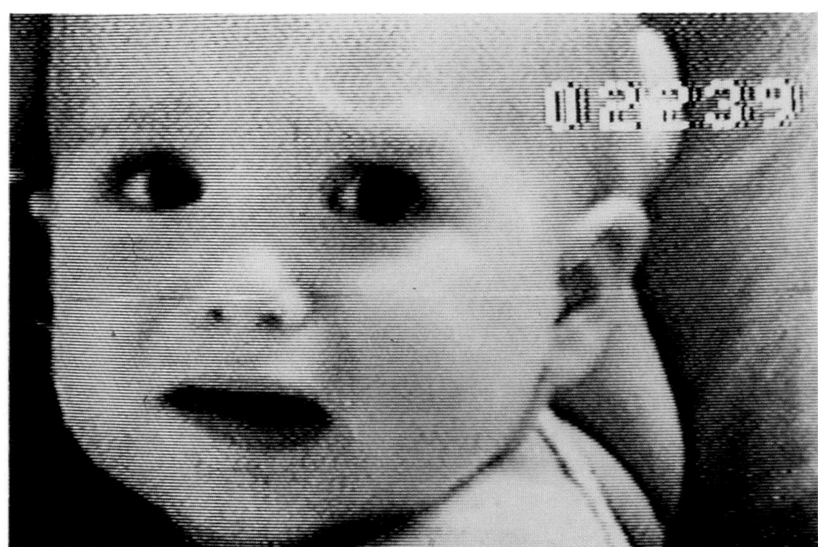

This baby is afraid.

This baby is sad.

Courtesy Carroll Izard, University of Delaware

Sometimes words just don't work.
It may be too noisy to use words, or too dangerous.
Maybe no one would hear the words or read them.
Some people might not understand the words.
Or maybe there just isn't time to use words.

For all the times that words don't work, people have figured out special signals to use instead.

When an American flag is upside down, it means help is needed.

These are the signals that bicycle riders give —

for left turn

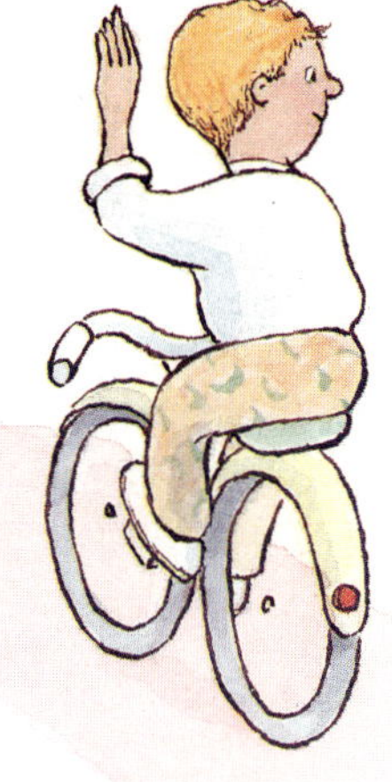

for right turn

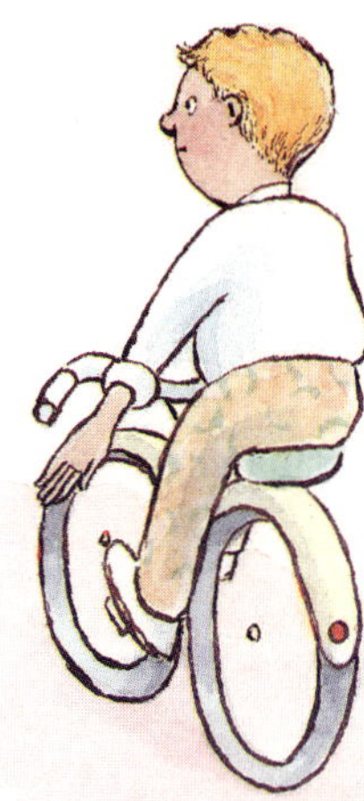

and for stop.

This signal tells the airplane pilot to stop.

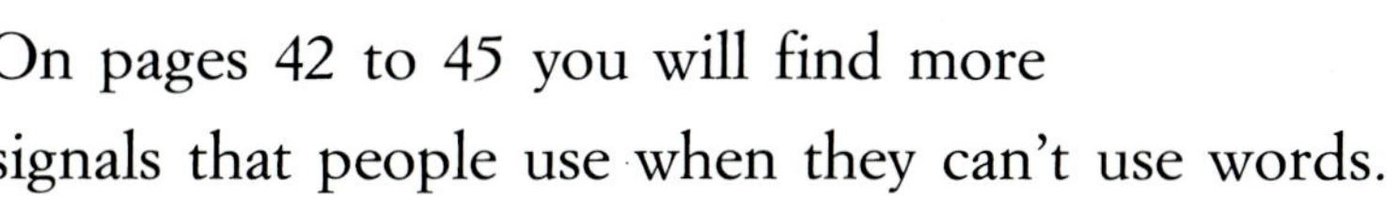

On pages 42 to 45 you will find more signals that people use when they can't use words.

Courtesy French Government Tourist Office

When people lived in caves thousands of years ago, they painted pictures on the walls of the caves. Maybe the pictures were stories the cave people wanted to tell. Nobody knows for sure.

Pictures are another good way
to say things without using words.
For people who cannot read
and people who cannot write,
pictures come in handy!

You could make a shopping list with pictures for somebody who cannot read.

Years ago, most people couldn't read.
When they traveled from one town to another,
pictures helped them find
the places they were looking for.

These days, people often go to countries
where they do not know the language.
So pictures still help them find
the places they are looking for.

Now we have *international symbols.*
They are used all over the world.
You don't have to know a foreign language to understand them.

The Indians who lived in America a long time ago made pictures everywhere. They made pictures on rocks and in caves, on buffalo skins and birch bark, on tepees and trees.

The Indians did not know how to write with words, but they could do almost anything with pictures. They used pictures to write letters. They used pictures to tell about hunting trips. They told stories about famous battles with pictures. They made peace treaties with pictures. They even wrote their names with pictures.

No wonder we say that the Indians were good at *picture-writing.*

This is how some Dakota Indians wrote their names with pictures, about 100 years ago.
At the bottom of the page the names are written in English. Can you match the English names with the pictures the Indians used?
Here is a hint. The Indian with the long hair is called Long Hair.
Look at the bottom of the page to see if you're right.

1. 2. 3. 4. 5.

The names in English are:

- Long Hair
- Spotted Face
- Chief Red Cloud
- Licks-With-His-Tongue
- Feather-on-His-Head
- Chief Big Road
- Running Antelope
- Big Voice
- Caught-the-Enemy
- Goes-Through-the-Camp
- Red Shirt

6.

7.

8.

9.

10.

11.

1. Spotted Face 2. Running Antelope 3. Long Hair 4. Feather-on-His-Head 5. Red Shirt 6. Caught-the-Enemy 7. Chief Red Cloud 8. Goes-Through-the-Camp 9. Chief Big Road 10. Big Voice 11. Licks-With-His-Tongue

Some Indian tribes also used picture-writing to remind them of important things that happened.

You can get an idea of what the Indians did if you think of a photo album you might make. Every year you would put just *one* picture in your album — a picture of something special that happened that year. Maybe it would be the time you started school, or learned to swim, or got the measles. Later on, the album would help you remember those years.

The Indians didn't have photo albums, of course. Every winter the oldest and wisest men in the tribe would get together and pick out something special that happened that year. Then one of the men would paint a little picture of it — usually on an animal skin. He painted it next to the picture he had painted the year before.

Sometimes the wise old men would take out the pictures and show them to the people of the tribe. They would tell the people the story of each picture. That way the tribe would always remember its history.

THAT'S THE YEAR I WAS BORN!

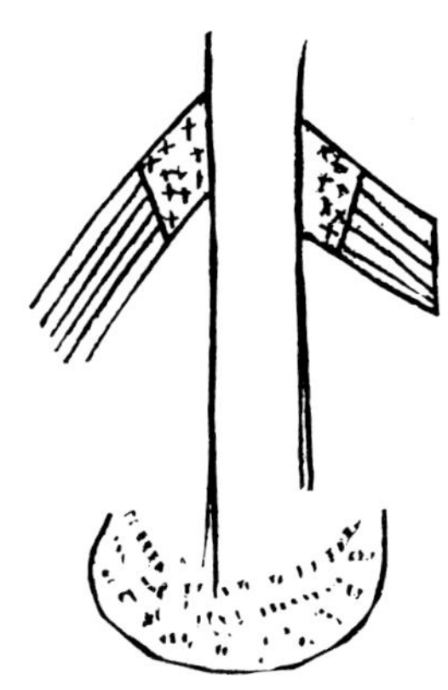

One year the white men met with the Indians and gave them flags as a sign of friendship. (The dots at the bottom are meant to be people.)

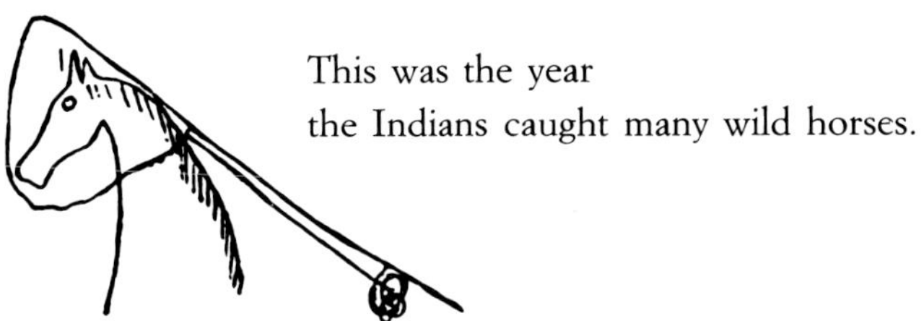

This was the year the Indians caught many wild horses.

The pictures also helped the Indians keep track of time. They knew there was one picture for every year. So two pictures in a row meant two years, five pictures meant five years, and ten pictures meant ten years.

If you wanted to know how old you were, you would find the picture for the year you were born. Then you would count the pictures that came after it. If there were 10 pictures, you were 10 years old.

The Indians would say you were "10 winters old," though. They counted in winters instead of in years. That is why their pictures of the years are called *winter counts.*

This picture reminded the Indians of the year a Dakota Indian named Brave Man was killed in a great fight.

This was the year Paints-His-Face-Red was killed in his tepee.

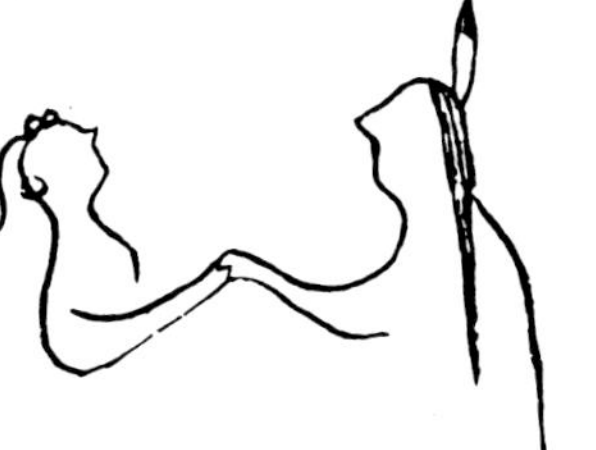

These three pictures all show the Indians making peace. The first picture tells about the time a Mandan Indian and a Dakota Indian met in the middle of the Missouri River and shook hands.

The only winter counts we know about
were made by Indians who lived on the Great Plains.
The pictures on these two pages are from their winter counts.

This is the year
there were many shooting stars.

The Indians drew this picture to help them remember the year the Dakotas and the Cheyennes were at war.

This picture reminded the Indians of the year everybody had the measles.

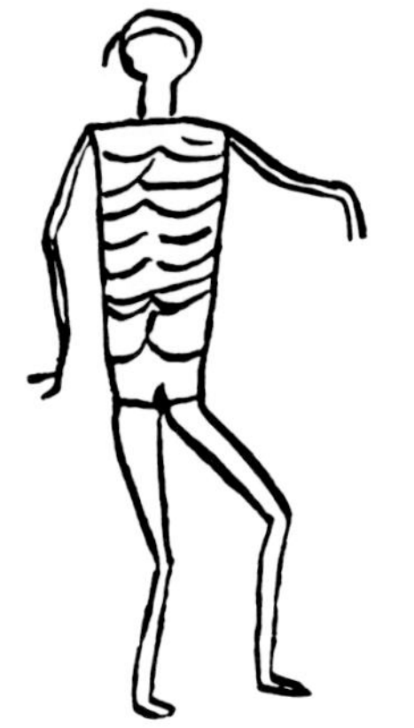

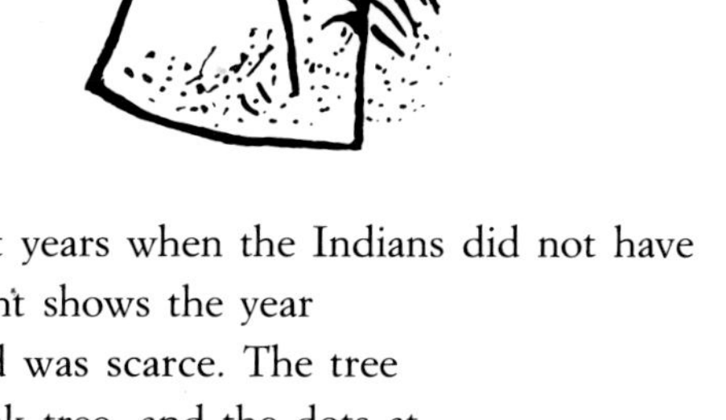

These pictures tell about two different years when the Indians did not have enough to eat. The picture on the right shows the year a tribe had to eat acorns because food was scarce. The tree in the picture is supposed to be an oak tree, and the dots at the bottom are meant to be acorns.

And this was the year the Indians had plenty of food. They drew a buffalo hide for that year to show they had lots of buffalo meat to eat.

Meaning: *If you are sick they will care for you.*

Meaning: *This is a good place for a handout.*

Meaning: *If you work she will feed you.*

A different kind of picture-writing was used by hoboes.

Hoboes were people who went from town to town on freight trains. They had no real homes and no real jobs. They jumped on the trains when nobody was looking, and when they got off they tried to find some work and some food.

Wherever they went, hoboes left secret messages for each other. The messages were written in *hobo signs* — a special kind of picture-writing. The signs said things like "You will get good food here" or "Stay away from this town!"

Hoboes left their messages where other hoboes would find them — on a kitchen door, maybe, or on a sidewalk or fence or wall.

Meaning: *Kind lady lives here.*

Meaning: *This is a good place to catch a train.*

Meaning: *Rich people live here.*

Meaning: *Danger!*

Meaning: *Get out of here quick!*

Meaning: *A good road to follow.*

There aren't many hoboes around now.
But there were lots of hoboes in America
up to the 1930s and 1940s.
There are some hobo signs on these two pages.
Hoboes usually made their signs with a piece of chalk or a crayon.

Meaning: *There is a doctor here who won't charge you.*

Meaning: *Man with gun lives here.*

Here are a few signs
that were put together to make longer messages.
Can you read the messages?

Kind lady lives here. If you work, she will feed you.

Danger. Man with a gun lives here. Get out of here quick!

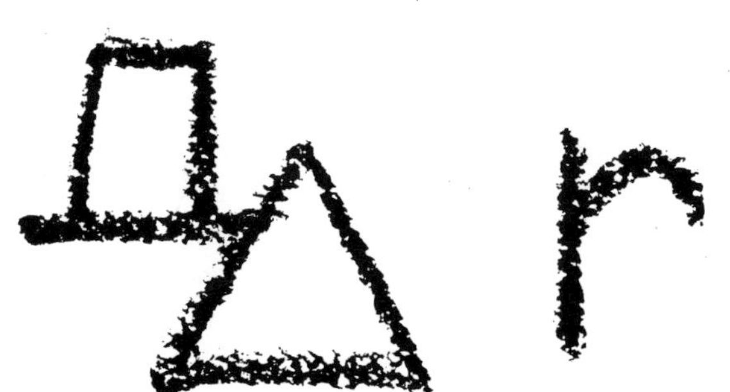

Rich people live here. If you are sick, they will take care of you.

You probably won't find any hobo signs
or Indian picture-writing except in museums or books.
But you are sure to see lots of other picture-writing
every day. It's all around you!

Here is some picture-writing you may see
on your way to school every morning.
All of these signs mean you are getting close to a school.

Most school signs show a big boy leading a little girl. But
on some signs, it's the other way around.

You can see some other road signs and highway signs on page 46.

If you go to school in a car,
you might see some more picture-writing
right on the dashboard.
Can you figure out what these pictures mean?

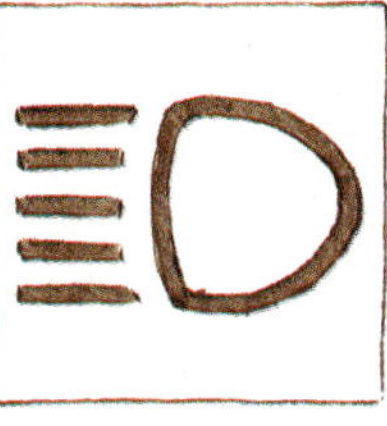

Lights

Fuel

Fasten seat belt

Heater

Horn

Oil

Fan

Radio

When you get home from school,
maybe there will be a package waiting for you.
A package with picture-writing on it
can go anywhere in the world.
Everybody will understand what the pictures mean.

This box came from a country where the people do not speak English. But on its way to your house, everyone could tell
they had to keep the box dry,
handle it as carefully as a glass,
and keep it right side up.

Something that you will see in more and more places
is a picture of a wheelchair. Maybe you have already
seen it on buildings and stores and restrooms.
The picture means that you can use these places easily
if you are on crutches or in a wheelchair or can't walk very well.

When this picture is
on the license plate of a car,
it usually means that the driver
of the car has trouble walking.
Most parking lots have a few spaces
marked with this picture
especially for these drivers.
Sometimes the car has special controls to help the driver.

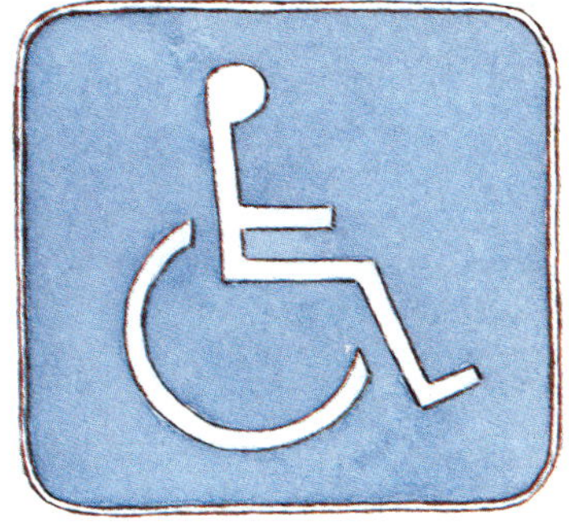

Now you know about some of the ways that people can say things to each other without using words.

Saying things without words means no *talking,* of course.
It also means no *writing.*
It even means not using the letters of the alphabet —
because words are made of letters.
Scientists have a special name for the ways
we say things without words.
The name is *non-verbal communication.*

This book does not talk about all the kinds
of non-verbal communication that people use.
Is music a kind of non-verbal communication?
It probably is. What about giving a flower to a friend?
There are many other ways to say things without words.
Everyone who reads this book is sure to think of some!

This part of the book has some extra information about the sign language of deaf people and the sign language of Indians. It also tells you more about some of the other things you have read about in this book.

Some of the signs that deaf people use are on pages 8 and 9. Here are some more.

Thank you

Yes

No

Girl

Boy

Cat

There are some Indian signs
on pages 10 and 11.
Here are some more.

Friend

Sleep

House

Owl

Tepee

River

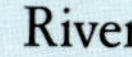

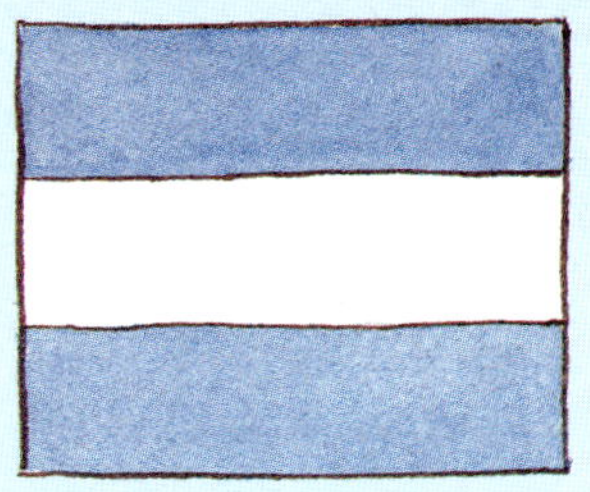

Meaning: *I am on fire and have dangerous cargo on board: keep well clear of me.*

The boat in the picture on page 23 is flying its flag upside down. That is a signal for HELP! It is one of the signals small American boats can use when they are in trouble.

Large vessels everywhere have a set of flags — called international code flags — they can use for sending messages. The messages are sent by raising one or more flags at a time.

Meaning: *Man overboard*

Meaning: *You are running into danger.*

Meaning: *I wish you a pleasant voyage.*

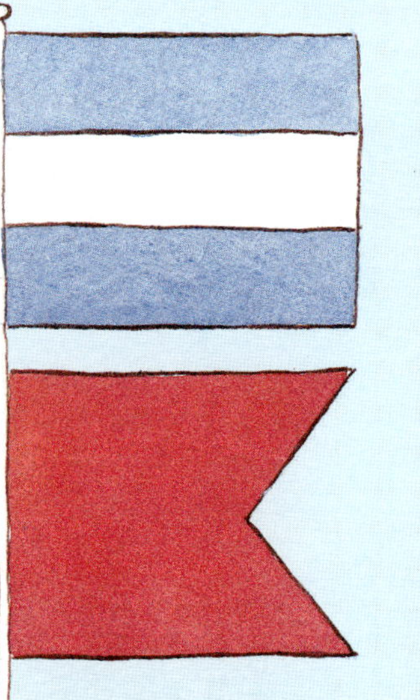

Meaning: *There is danger of explosion.*

Meaning: *I require assistance.*

Meaning: *I require immediate assistance.*

Meaning: *I require immediate assistance; I have sprung a leak.*

The signal to an airplane pilot to stop the plane is on page 23. Here are more signals that are used when an airplane is on the ground. At night, the person giving the signals has a special light in each hand.

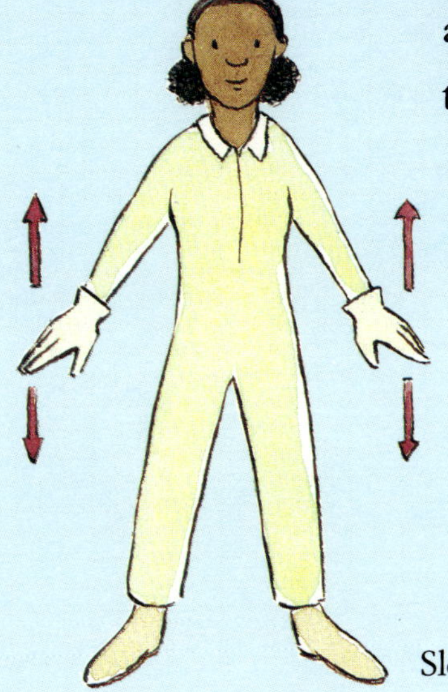

Slow down.

Move forward.

Shut down the engine.

Other signals that people use at work are shown below and on the next two pages.

The people who make TV and radio programs have to be quiet when they tell the actors what to do. Here are some of the signals they use.

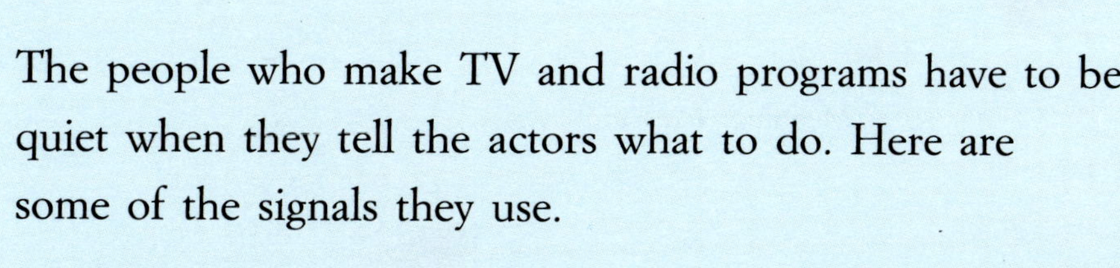

Hurry up.

Cut!

When a building is going up, someone has to tell the crane operator what to do. Here are some of the signals the workers use.

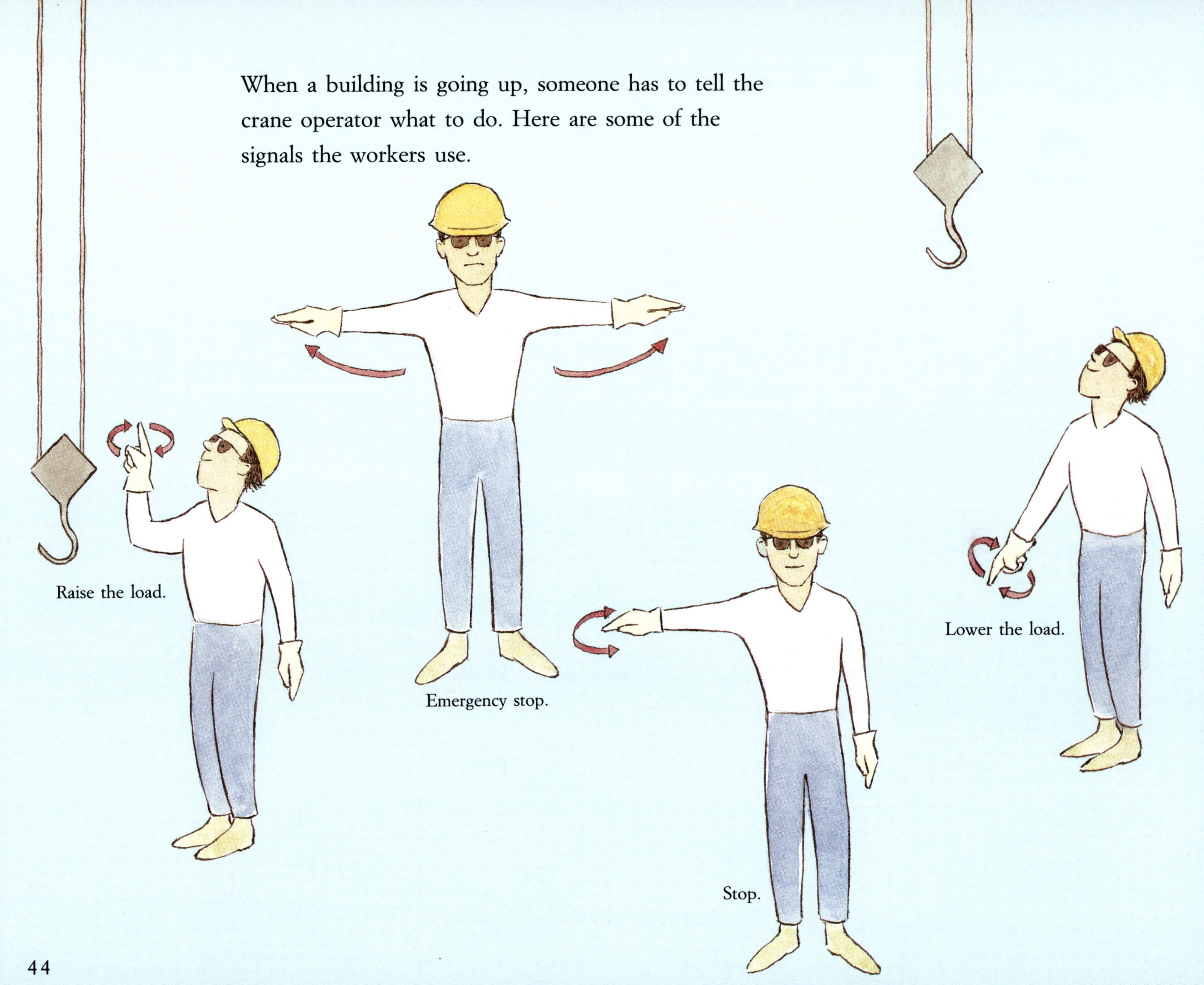

Raise the load.

Emergency stop.

Stop.

Lower the load.

In many sports, the players tell each other things secretly — with secret signals.

This catcher is telling the pitcher to throw a breaking pitch.

Referees don't have to talk either.

This referee is warning a soccer player by showing him a yellow card. If the referee holds up a red card, the player is out of the game.

On page 36 there are pictures that mean *school.* Here are some other signs that you might see on streets, roads, and highways. A line through the picture means *not allowed.*

And here are some other signs and symbols you see very often.

You don't need words!

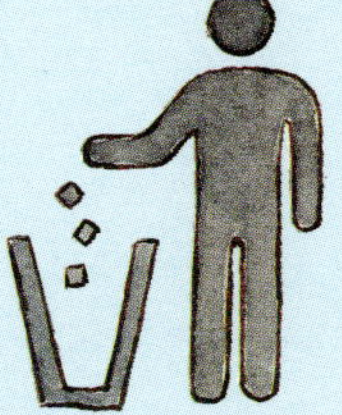